ANDALUSIA

ENGLISH EDITION

© OTERMIN EDICIONES, S.C.
Telf. & Fax: (95) 229 56 42
ISBN. 84-88187-63-7
Dep. Legal: MA. 691-98

TRANSLATOR:
ADRIENNE BAILLIE

Almeria

Seville

Huelva

Seville

Granada

Jaen

Whitewashed wall, Malaga

Cactus, Almeria

Almeria

Geraniums

INTRODUCTION

Andalusia is situated in the southernmost part of the Iberian Peninsula. It is the largest of all the Spanish autonomous regions, having an area of 87,268 square kilometres and a population of approximately 6,500,000. The eight provinces which make up this region are: **Almeria, Cadiz, Cordoba, Granada, Huelva, Jaen, Malaga and Seville.**

The geographical structure of Andalusia is typically Mediterranean, with three different orographic regions, which from north to south are: the Sierra Morena, a range of mountains which crosses Andalusia from east to west, acting as a natural border with the Castilian plateau; the Guadalquivir valley, triangular in shape, which lies between the Sierra Morena and the Bética mountains and through which the river Guadalquivir passes, collecting water from the Sierra Morena and from the larger part of the Bética mountains; the third area is the Bética mountain range, occupying almost half of the Andalusian territory, along the Mediterranean coast from Cape Gata in Almeria, to Gibraltar. Ronda, Las Alpujarras and Sierra Nevada all form part of this range of mountains. The highest point in the Iberian Peninsula, the Mulhacen (3,481 metres), is to be found in Sierra Nevada.

Andalusia has the warmest climate in Spain, typically Mediterranean, hot and dry in summer, with mild winters. The average yearly temperature is 16° Celsius inland, and 18°C on the Mediterranean coast.

We have proof of Man's presence in Andalusia from at least one million years ago, in the Quaternary period. His skills then would have been limited to chipping a stone to a sharp point or edge, for self defence and hunting. The oldest human remains found in Andalusia date from 80,000 years ago: the Neanderthal Homo (first stage of Homo sapiens). These early settlers sought safety and shelter in caves and gradually learned the use of fire. There is extensive evidence of the presence of Homo sapiens in Andalusia. It would appear these people came to Spain from Africa through the Strait of Gibraltar, which in the Quaternary period could be crossed on foot.

At the end of the last Ice Age when the ice disappeared, those animals which were the main source of food for these early hunters also disappeared. The Paleolithic came to an end, giving way to the Neolithic Age in which man underwent marked changes: from being a simple predator he starts to apply his knowledge of Nature and collaborate with her. During the last part of the 5th millennium BC he progresses from a nomadic food gatherer, to a food producer. Agriculture probably came to Europe from Africa via Andalusia.

With the emergence of the metal culture, a big improvement became apparent in tools, arms and other implements. The Andalusian mountain area, rich in gold, silver, copper and other metals, soon occupied a privileged trading position.

Sailors from the east developed ambitious plans for travel routes and colonizing in Andalusia to protect their commerce: contemporary competitors, such as the Phoenicians and Greeks, also came to this area and were a decisive factor in the history of Southern Andalusia. At the same time, the Kingdom of Tartessos starts to show signs of solid political unity, taking over the mineral resources and growing rich with the profits from overseas trade, at the same time exploiting extensive areas in cattle and farming.

The history of the period between the 6th and 3rd centuries BC is one on which we have only scarce information. We do know of the important role of the Carthaginians in ensuring the safety of their trade routes with the support of a powerful army.

From the middle of the 3rd century BC Rome and Carthage were at open war. The control of the west was in dispute. After their first major defeat the Carthaginians decided to reduce occupation to those territories farthest away from Rome. In 237 BC **Hamilcar**, the Carthaginian general, landed in Cadiz and over the next 10 years took control of all the south and southeastern territories in Iberia. By then Tartessos had been divided into several kingdoms, with varying degrees of power, which kept to their original activities in the fields of economy, art, and culture. In an attempt to restrain the Carthaginians, the Romans signed the Treaty of the Ebro, but **Hannibal**, Hamilcar's son, attacked Sagunto, thus initiating the second war between Rome and Carthage.

The struggle for political control between Rome and Carthage was at its most virulent in the Iberian Peninsula. In 206 BC the Roman general, **Scipio**, nick-named ***the African***, conquered the region which he named Bética, after the River Baetis (now Guadalquivir). Romanization began and the use of Latin, in those days the language of cultural exchange. Philosophers such as **Seneca** and the first emperors born outside the Roman Peninsula, such as **Trajan** and **Hadrian**, came from this Roman province.

With Roman occupation, the Iberian people became an integral part of historical Mediterranean culture. The Romans built roads to permit the movement of their legions and traders, settling camps and building cities which became important trade centres.

Around 411 AD, the Barbarians from the far side of the Rhine arrived in Andalusia. They crossed the Strait of Gibraltar and occupied the African coastline. Later, in 458 AD, they would be replaced by the Visigoths. These settlers, intermarrying with the Spanish-Roman aristocracy, formed the first monarchy in Andalusia.

In the year 711 AD an Arab-Berber army of some 12,000 men under **Tarik** defeated the King of the Visigoths, **Rodrigo**, on the banks of the River Guadalete in Cadiz; at this point the history of Al-Andalus begins. After an arduous siege, **Tarik** occupied **Cordoba** and followed the Roman roads, conquering **Toledo**.

One year later, a new army occupied **Carmona, Seville** and **Merida.** In 716 AD most of the Spanish-Visigoth population were permitted to keep their properties in exchange for the payment of taxes. The victors, some 30,000 Arabs and Berbers, were given land, thus initiating Islamic settlement in Al-Andalus.

Al-Andalus is the name given by the Arabs to their new domains and is the origin of the word Andalusia. Al-Andalus was to become the centre of Muslim Spain; here a new civilization was formed, where different cultures and religions would intermingle.

Granada   Jaen   Malaga

Cadiz   Jaen

Cadiz

Granada   Cordoba

In the year 755 AD **Abd-al-Rahman** declared the first independent Emirate. Society then was very homogenous and along with the political and economic aristocracy, small traders, craftsmen and farmers enjoyed the prosperity of the period.

In 922 AD Al-Andalus reached a peak of cultural and economic splendour. During the Caliphate, **Cordoba** was to become the city with the largest population in all Occident.

In the 10th century AD the "**Muladies**" (Muslims of Spanish origin), resentful of the ethnic discrimination, religious pluralism and regional differences, began a movement for independence. This was during the Omayyad monarchy of Cordoba, and the result was the disintegration of Al-Andalus into different Taifa kingdoms. In spite of being weak militarywise, these kingdoms, being very strong culturally, gave rise to the most splendid period of the history of Muslim Spain.

During the 11th and 12th centuries new Muslim invasions occurred under the **Almoravids** and **Almohads:** conquest for these was easy because of the Taifa kingdoms' military weakness. Only the kingdom of **Seville**, under the Berbers, and the Kingdom of **Granada**, maintained their historical continuity.

After the Battle of **Navas de Tolosa**, in 1212, and the conquests of **King Ferdinand III** of Castile, Al-Andalus became part of the Kingdom of Castile. The exception was Granada, which would only be conquered in 1492, by the Catholic Monarchs **King Ferdinand** and **Queen Isabella** (*Los reyes católicos Isabel y Fernando*). Granada held a privileged position as it was on the route by which Sudanese gold reached Castile. This gold was traded by the **Nasrids** in exchange for oil, cloth and weapons. The Kingdom of the Nasrids could only hold out because of Castilian tolerance due to their interest in maintaining the taxes paid by Granada.

During the seven centuries of Arab civilization in Spain, their influence in linguistics, farming, science and art was enormous. The Arabs introduced a whole range of technical, botanical and economical innovations. Some examples are: the watermill, paper, the cultivation of the silkworm. A whole new wide range of perfumes and flavours previously unknown to the European continent was also introduced, such as jasmine, saffron, rice, sugar, apricots, lemons, watermelons and aubergines.

From the 13th century on, and as a result of the conquests of **Ferdinand III** and **Alfonso X**, the prosperous intensive farming in the Guadalquivir Valley was to be exploited to the full, with olives and cattle as the main stay. With the growth of Turkish power, fear arose that Granada would be the possible point of entry for a new Muslim invasion of Europe. In a period of only eleven years, the Catholic Monarchs were to conquer all the territories of the Kingdom of Granada, a conquest which concluded with the surrender of **Boabdil**, King of Granada.

During the 13th century, the Christian majority co-existed with the Jewish and **Mudejar** minorities. Both of these minorities were subject to discriminatory laws however, and obliged to pay special taxes.

In the 14th century, trade routes to north Africa and the Canary Islands were opened up, with the result of a marked increase in commerce in Andalusia. There were three reasons for this: the geographic position of **Seville** permitted boats of up to 300 tons access to the sea via the Guadalquivir River. Tonnage increased in the 15th century and ports such as **Sanlucar de Barrameda, Puerto de Santa Maria** and **Cadiz** became increasingly important. Another reason was the agricultural richness of Andalusia in such products as oil, cereals, chickpeas, leather, wool, honey, skins, cheese and wine. A third and decisive factor was the existence of a rich nobility and merchants who were in control of foreign trade.

There were various Atlantic routes to Seville: the coastal route with Portugal (wine, wheat and figs in exchange for cork and fruits) and that with Portugal's African territories, the Cantabrian route which in the 15th century allowed commerce with the Galician, Cantabrian and Basque people (fish, iron and wood were traded for oil, cereal and wine).

Atlantic Andalusia soon became the most important economic region of the Kingdom of Castile. This encouraged agricultural production, the investing of capital, work was created and the knowledge of maritime routes was enormously improved.

The different cultures which had in turn left their mark on this land have contributed to the creation of an individualistic, open and hospitable people who have throughout centuries assimilated a rich and varied knowledge and culture.

Lagoon with flamencos, Fuente de Piedra, Malaga.

ALMERIA

This eastern Andalusian province is made up mostly of two mountain ranges: the Sub Betica range in the north and the Penibetica in the south, separated from each other by the Almanzor valley. The coastal mountains of Gata, Cabrera and Almagrera towards the east end in high cliffs, whereas in the south, from Cape Gata onwards the coastline is flat and sandy, opening out on to the Bay of Almeria.

The climate of this province is very dry. Rains are scarce and the mean yearly temperature is 18°C. Winters are mild, with 12°C as an average, whereas summers are very hot with an average of 24°C. In the highest parts of the mountains temperatures can be as low as minus 13°C. Vegetation is sub-tropical, consisting of drought-resistant species: Pita, cactus and palm shoots, although in the highest mountains there are pines and holm oak.

The mineral richness here was the origin of the prehistoric settlements such as those of "Los Millares" and "El Argar". The city of **Almeria** is of Phoenician origin, the founders called this port city *"Urci"*, and it was the centre of their metal trade. Its importance increased with the arrival of the Romans and the city was renamed *"Portus Magnus"*.

The peak of splendour of Almeria came with the arrival of the Arab, especially with the Cordoba Omayyad Emirate. The Arabs called the city *Al-Miriya* (the mirror), thus giving Almeria its present name. In the reign of **Abderraman III**, the city grew in size and at the fall of the Cordoba Emirate, when **Almanzor** died, it became an independent emirate which through the 11th century spread to include parts of **Granada, Cordoba, Jaen** and **Murcia.**

Almeria was then one of the richest cities in Europe after **Cordoba** and **Constantinople.** In 1147 **Alfonso VII** of Castile conquered the city and the kingdom.

Almeria

La Alcazaba

La Alcazaba

The Cathedral

Interior of the Cathedral

Urbanización Playa Serena. Roquetas de Mar

Santa Ana castle, 16thc, Roquetas de Mar

Bull ring, Roquetas de Mar

Roquetas de Mar

Sports Marina at Almerimar, El Ejido

Beach at Aguadulce

Laujar de Andarax, capital of Almerian La Alpujarra

Beach at Aguamarga, Níjar

El Arco beach, Los Escullos

Isleta del Moro, Níjar

Isleta del Moro, Níjar

Playa de Los Muertos. Carboneras

Playazo Rodalquilar, Níjar. Nature Park of Cabo de Gata-Níjar

Nature Park of Cabo de Gata-Níjar

Beach at Monsul, San José, Níjar. Nature Park of Cabo de Gata-Níjar

Ten years later however, the Arabs reconquered Almeria. In 1489 Ferdinand and Isabella, the Catholic Monarchs (***los Reyes Católicos Isabel y Fernando***) finally took the city. From then on, a period of economic decline started in **Almeria**, aggravated by the expulsion of the *moriscos* (Arabs who had accepted Christian baptism). The fields were left abandoned despite the fact that Christian re-settlers came from all over Spain. Until 1822, Almeria formed part of the so-called Kingdom of Granada, when Parliament determined the province boundaries,which have been maintained up to this day. **Almeria** started to recover its demographic and economic importance in the 19th century, with the establishment of the Gador mines, which resulted in the arrival of the railway and construction of the port. **Mojacar** and **Roquetas de Mar** are two historic-touristic cities of this province.

La Alcazaba, the most important monument in **Almeria**, dates from the Muslim occupation. It was built by **Abderraman III** in the 7th century and extended by **Almanzor** in the 10th c. It stands on top of a hill from which the bay and the whole city can be seen. The Cathedral is a typical example of late Gothic temple-fortress, built in the period 1524-1543. On the façade, four large stone towers stand out, other important details are the two main doors, the choir, the sacristy, the transept, and the High Altar with its different chapels. Other important monuments are the churches of Santiago el Viejo, San Pedro and San Juan.

The **Gata-Nijar Nature Park** lies a few km. to the east of the capital. Created in 1987, it has an area of some 29,000 hectares. It occupies part of the **Almeria, Carboneras** and **Nijar** municipalities, and has a shoreline of bays, cliffs, reefs and white sandy beaches.

Los Genoveses beach, San José. Níjar. Nature Park of Cabo de Gata-Níjar

Sports Marina, San José, Níjar

Waterwheel, Pozo de Los Frailes

San José, Níjar

Níjar pueblo

Handcraft in Níjar Pueblo

Pueblo de Tabernas

Panoramic view of the town of Sorbas

Artistic pottery, Sorbas

General view of the town of Mojácar

Typical Mojácar street

Playa de El Cantal, Mojácar

Architectural detail, Mojácar

Pueblo Indalo, Mojácar

Club Marina Golf, Mojácar

Playa Cueva del Lobo, Mojácar

Playa Marina de la Torre, Mojácar

Torre de Macenas, 18th c. Mojácar

Garrucha fishing port

Garrucha

Las Marinas-Bolaga beach, Vera

Serón

Vélez Blanco

Sierra María-Los Vélez Nature Park

Sierra María-Los Vélez Nature Park

C A D I Z

The province of **Cadiz** is situated on the southern vertex of the Iberian Peninsula; its eastern shore is bathed by the Mediterranean Sea, the western shore by the Atlantic Ocean.

There are three large geographical regions: to the east, a mountainous area defined by Grazalema and Ubrique and coastal Tarifa; to the north we have the marshes and at the coastline we find two important bays: the **Bay of Cadiz**, a low sandy bay with many dunes caused by the winds from the Atlantic, and **the Bay of Algeciras**, on the Strait of Gibraltar.

Three rivers flow through the province to the Atlantic: the Guadalquivir, Guadalete and Barbate. The Guadiaro flows into the Mediterranean between Cadiz and Malaga.

Because of its southern position in the Iberian Peninsula, **Cadiz** played an important part in history as a bridge between Europe and Africa and a gateway to the Atlantic.

Cadiz is one of the oldest of the Western cities, dating back more than 3,000 years. It was a prosperous Carthaginian colony before the Roman invasion and one of the most important trade ports, being a compulsory stopping off place for all ships en route to the Atlantic from the Mediterranean; this favoured trade with the Guadalquivir Valley. The prosperity of **Cadiz** (*Cádiz, Gades, Gadir*) was maintained throughout the Roman period,

Beach at La Caleta, Cadiz

Genoves Park

Monument to Moret

Detail: Puerta de Tierra

La Victoria Beach

Valderrama Golf Course, Sotogrande

Sotogrande

Leisure port at Sotogrande, San Roque, on the Guadiaro

Lighthouse at Trafalgar

Port of Barbate

Los Caños de Meca

Tarifa Beach

Los Caños de Meca

Bay of Bolonia

Water sports on the Western Coast

but was interrupted at the time of the Muslim invasion, when a frontier running through the villages on the plains was settled, facing the mountain area of the Kingdom of Granada. Some villages still keep their nickname *"la frontera"* (the frontier) such as in **Arcos de la Frontera, Chiclana de la Frontera, Jerez de la Frontera** or **Vejer de la Frontera.**

Cadiz was finally reconquered in 1265, but did not recover its trade prosperity until the 16th c when it became the port for important trade with the Americas. In 1558, ships coming from the Antilles with cargoes of leathers and sugar were allowed to unload in Cadiz. Permission to enter port was also granted to all ships arriving with technical problems incurred during their Atlantic voyage which prevented their crossing the sandbar barrier at the entrance to the Guadalquivir River en route to Seville. This determined the prominence of **Cadiz,** especially when goods from America started arriving in larger ships. Foreign traders also realised that the port of **Cadiz** offered more facilities than the port of **Seville.**

Beach at Cape Trafalgar

We understand then why when the Plague reached Europe in the middle of the 17th century, devastating **Cadiz** and **Seville**, the latter began a slow and lasting decline, whereas **Cadiz** quickly recovered from this crisis. On the invasion by the French at the beginning of the 19th century, Parliament was transferred to **Cadiz** by Government decree in 1811. This was an positive period for the Parliament. The Government started by proclaiming national sovereignty, incorporating the judicial counties into the nation and abolishing feudalism. Laws were also drafted on printing, censorship abolished and the Inquisition suppressed. The political Constitution of the Spanish Monarchy was drawn up.

The most important monument in **Cadiz** is its Cathedral. Building was started in 1720. It has three naves, with lateral chapels, transept, dome and Girola (central nave with apse). Other important churches are: Santa Cruz, Santo Domingo, Carmen and San Agustin. The archaeological museum contains a wide variety of prehistoric remains, as well as items from Carthaginian, Greek and Roman cultures, and Early Christian and Visigoth cultures.

Cities to visit in the province are: **Algeciras, Arcos de la Frontera, la Linea, Puerto de Santa María, San Fernando, Sanlucar de Barrameda, Tarifa** and **Vejer.**

The **Nature Park of Barbate**, a maritime terrestrial park, is situated on the Atlantic coast at the entry to the Strait of Gibraltar. The marshlands along the Barbate River serve as a resting place for many migratory birds.

The **Bay of Cadiz**, declared a National Park in 1989, has an extension of 10,000 hectares and consists of beaches and marshlands originated by fluvial sediments. Its important fauna includes many migratory birds. UNESCO has declared the **Nature Park Sierra de Grazalema** a Biosphere Reserve. It has an extension of some 51,000 hectares and is situated to the west of the Bética mountains, extending through the mountain area of Cadiz and through part of the Serrania of Ronda in the province of Malaga.

The **Nature Park of Los Alcornocales** has an area of 170,000 h., extending from **Tarifa** in the south to the northwest of Malaga. It has the largest wood of cork trees in the Iberian Peninsula, which is also one of the most important in size in the world.

Sanlucar de Barrameda

Zahara de las Atunes

Arcos de la Frontera

La Cartuja, Jerez

Cathedral, Jerez

Church of San Miguel, Jerez

Royal Andalusian School of Equestrian Art, Jerez de la Frontera

Gonzalez Byass Wine Cellars, Jerez de la Frontera

CORDOBA

The Province of **Cordoba**, through which the middle course of the Guadalquivir River flows, is the northernmost of the eight Andalusian provinces. Outstanding geographical points are the Sierra Morena to the north, La Campiña in the centre and the Sub-Bética range of mountains in the south. Since the province is surrounded by mountains and there is no moderating maritime influence, its climate is combined Mediterranean and Continental. Mean yearly temperatures reach about 19°C with winters averaging 10°C, whereas summers are extremely hot, when temperatures can often reach 45°C and above.

The city of **Cordoba** is situated on the banks of the Guadalquivir River and has always been an important crossroads. Roads to **Extremadura**, heading west across the Sierra, the route to the Meseta, crossing the Sierra Morena through **Despeñaperros**, and the Via Augusta, which ran along the Guadalquivir up to **Cadiz**, through **Seville**, all converge here. The location of **Cordoba**, in the Bética Valley where the Sierra and La Campiña meet, determined its importance as a trading and cultural centre in this region.

The capital city of **Cordoba** was founded by the Carthaginians. Its epoch of splendour began around 169 BC when **Claudius Marcellus** settled a Roman colony there. **Cordoba**'s strategic position and rich agriculture contributed to its extensive development. By 584 AD it had become a meeting point for Visigoths and Byzantines.

Roman bridge over the Guadalquivir, Cordoba

The Mosque-Cathedral, interior

The Mosque-Cathedral, interior

In 716 AD, and now under Muslim occupation, **Cordoba** became the capital of **Al-Andalus**. By 756 AD it was the Emirate capital and in 929 AD the capital of the Caliphate. This led to an extensive growth,the city occupying a larger area than today. It was the most populated Western city, with more than 250,000 inhabitants. By comparison, **Toledo** had 37,000 inhabitants, **Almeria** 27,000, **Granada** 26,000, **Zaragoza** 17,000 and **Valencia** and **Malaga** some 15,000 inhabitants. The urban organization was apparent in all Muslim cities. The public granary, the *alcaicería,* markets and public baths were situated around the Mosque (*La Mezquita Mayor).*

Economic activity was based on farming and cattle raising. Cereal and pulse foods were cultivated and surpluses of olives, raisins and figs were exported to the East. By the 10th century windmills and watermills were in use and rice, oranges and sugarcane were cultivated and exported.

Crafts included the manufacture of gold jewelry, and ivory and jade carvings. In the 11th century two new industries appeared: paper and glass. The process of glass manufacture was kept secret, allowing Al-Andalus to maintain a monopoly in the production of a certain type of glass for several centuries. The Muslim culture in Spain was comparable to that of the Eastern Muslim countries. The Caliphate library held over 400.000 volumes.

The most important monument of the Muslim occupation is the Grand Mosque, the *Mezquita Mayor*. Building started around 780 AD under **Abd-Rahman** and was completed by **Almanzor** who added 8 new naves on the East side. At present the Mosque occupies a rectangle of 180 m. north to south, and 130 m. east to west. Most of its columns come from previous Roman, early Christian and Visigoth buildings. On the conquest of the city in 1236 by **Ferdinand III,** the Christian re-consagration and transformation of the Mezquita into a Cathedral brought changes to the interior of the Mosque, such as the construction of the Royal Chapel, wall chapels, and the adaptation of the skylight.

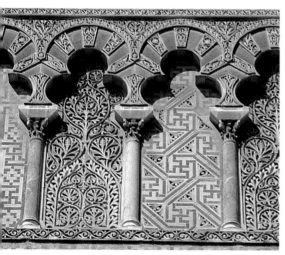

Details of interior of the Mosque Cathedral

Details of interior of the Mosque-Cathedral

Other important monuments in the city of **Cordoba** are: the Catholic Monarchs' *Alcazabar*, built by **Alfonso XI** in 1328 and the Synagogue, also built by **Alfonso XI** in 1315. This synagogue is one of only three existing in Spain and the only one in Andalusia.

Lucena, Montilla and **Puente Genil** are other cities of historic importance.

The **Nature Park of Cardeña and Montoro** belongs to Sierra Morena and is located at the northeast end of the Cordoba province. One of the characteristics of this park is *"Las Bolas",* heaps of rounded granite blocks with diameters of around one metre. **The Nature Park of Hornachuelos** lies in the west of the province. Its name comes from the dark colour of its slate soil. It has an area of 67,000 hectares, and species such as the black stork and the Iberian lynx form part of the local fauna.

Central nave, prayer room, Mosque

Statues of Ferdinand and Isabella, and Columbus

Castle Gardens

Castle gardens

Fountain

Plaza de las Flores

Typical patio in Cordoba

Wrought Iron window bars

Interiors of the Viana Palace-museum

The Alvear Winecellars, Montilla

Madinat al-Zahr

GRANADA

Granada province is situated between the provinces of **Malaga** and **Almeria,** adjacent to the provinces of **Jaen, Albacete and Murcia** to the north and **Cordoba** to the west with coastline on the Mediterranean sea. Near the present-day city of **Granada** was the Iberian city of Elvira, which became the capital of one of the Al-Andalus provinces up till the Berber revolt in 1009-1010. The population was then forced to emigrate to lands near **Granada**, settling in the Alhambra and Albaicin hills and in the plains around the Darro and Genil rivers.

After the fall of the Omayyad Caliphate of Cordoba came the reign of the *Zaries* of **Granada** and at the end of the 11th century the **Almoravids** took control of this kingdom, which would later be taken over by the **Almohads.** When the Almohad dynasty fell into decadence, a member of the **Ben-al-Ahman** family conquered **Granada** in 1238, initiating the **Nasrid** dynasty which would be in power for over two and a half centuries and whose kingdom extended all the way to the provinces of **Malaga** and **Almeria.**

Many of the Muslims who escaped from the reclaimed Castilian territories came here to repopulate this new kingdom. This area would be the last region in the Iberian Peninsula to be under Muslim rule. **Granada** developed into a large and rich city with several mosques, and palaces such as the **Alhambra.** The wealth of the Nasrid kingdom was ensured by the silk industry developed there, as well as its commerce with the East and with

Granada

La Alhambra

Interior details of the Alhambra

Patio de los Leones, Alhambra

Gardens of the Generalife

Southern facade of the Cathedral

Interior of the Cathedral

many of the Mediterranean countries of the north of Africa. Gold mined in the Sudan came through the trade routes into Europe via Granada.

After the **Capitulations of Granada** in 1492, when the Catholic Monarchs took power, few changes were expected in this region, as conditions agreed on allowed the peoples of Granada to keep their possessions, laws, customs and religion, and their rule over part of the city. But the agreements were violated and six years later two separate zones were established, one Christian, the other Muslim (the *Morería*). After the 1568 rebellion, the *Moriscos,* controllers of the silk industry, were expelled from the Albaicin.

In the time of the **Nasrids** (1241–1492) **Granada** reached its period of maximum splendour. The monuments which best represent that period are the **Alhambra**, the most important Muslim Palace remaining today, and the **Generalife**, which was the royal family's summer residence. An example of the fortress and military architecture is the Puerta de Elvira, the entrance to the walled city, built in the 13th c. The **Alcazaba** dates from the 13th century and the **Alcazar** from the 14th c. The Catholic Monarchs started an important artistic centre; this was continued by **Carlos V** who ordered the building of a palace within the Alhambra itself. One outstanding monument is the Cathedral, one of the most important examples of Renaissance art. Representative of the civil buildings is the Royal Hospital, founded in 1504. The main museums are the Alhambra Archaeological Museum, the Fine Arts Museum and the Municipality and Cathedral museums.

Royal Chapel, Cathedral

43

The Cartuja. Church

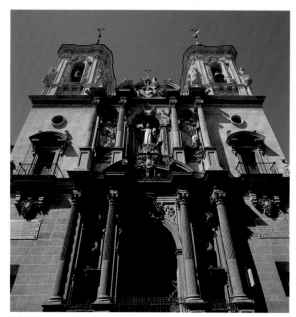

Main facade: Basilica of San Juan de Dios

Basilica of San Juan de Dios

There are many other religious monuments: the Gothic-Mudejar Church of San José, built on the remains of a mosque, la Cartuja, the Church of San Juan de Dios, and the Monastery of San Jerónimo.

Baza, Guadix, Motril and **Orjiva** are other historical municipalities of Granada.

To the east of the province, near Almeria, there is the **Nature Park of Sierra de Baza,** part of the Bética range of mountains. With altitudes varying from 1,200 to 2,000 m. this mountain area has a vegetation well adapted to high winds and low temperatures.

The **National Park of Sierra Nevada** has an area of some 170,000 h., occupying a large part of the Granada province and part of Almeria. It lies at the centre of the Penibetica range and is the largest mountain area of the Iberian Peninsula with an independent structural unity. In this Park there are more than 20 peaks over 3,000 m., the highest of which (also the highest in the Iberian Peninsula) is the Mulhacen at 3,481 metres. These heights are only surpassed in Europe by the Alps.

District of the Albayzín

La Alpujarra. Pampaneira. Bubión. Capileira

La Alpujarra

Sierra Nevada

La Calahorra

Guadix. District of the Caves

Salobreña

Almuñecar

Almuñecar

HUELVA

Huelva is the most western of the Andalusian provinces. Towards the west lies the border with **Portugal** and to the north, the border with **Extremadura**. **Seville** and **Cadiz** lie to the east and southeast, and the Atlantic borders the south. The province is situated between the Rivers Tinto and Odiel. Though **Huelva** is situated in what is known as "Dry Iberia", its Atlantic coastline allows for some relative humidity. Its main agricultural regions are on the plains, where cereals, vines and olive trees grow.

Primitive Mediterranean peoples settled in Huelva. Later, Huelva became an important commercial area for both Phoenicians and Carthaginians, and its mines of copper and iron pyrites were already exploited by them (at **Calañas, Rio Tinto** and **Tarsis)**.

In the Muslim occupation of Andalusia, two Taifa kingdoms were founded here, **Niebla** and **Huelva** being the main centres. By the middle of the 13th century the Castilians had reconquered Andalusia and established the southern frontiers in the Peninsula, restraining Lusitanian expansion to the East. Huelva was originally a land of miners and farmers but its people would soon become sailors, witnessing the discovery and conquest of the Americas. Though the first expeditions under **Christopher Columbus** set off from this coast, the commercial routes later established with America did not pass through here but instead followed the Guadalquivir river up to Seville. This part of Andalusia would lose importance up till the 19th c, when mining of mineral ores on a large scale was introduced.

Matalascañas Beach

Church of La Concepción

Monastery of la Rabida, interior

Pilgrimage of El Rocio

Ayamonte

Ayamonte

Canela Beach

Bridge over the Guadiana River

Geraniums by the Guadiana

Alajar, Sierra de Aracena

Matalascañas Beach

Bullfighting

Bullring at Huelva

National Park of Doñana

In 1257 **Alfonso X** reconquered Huelva and passed it to his daughter, **Doña Beatriz de Gúzman**, the widowed Queen of Portugal. In the 15th century it returned to Spanish control. The territories of Huelva were integrated into the administration of the Kingdom of Seville up till 1833, when the present day frontiers were established, which added part of the Kingdom of Seville and a small part of Extremadura.

Palos de la Frontera is the Huelva port from which **Columbus** set sail on his voyage of discovery of the Americas; it is 11 km. from the capital city **Huelva.** Nearby one can see the Monastery of **La Rabida**.

The 18th century earthquakes destroyed many of the buildings in Huelva city, so there are relatively few monuments. We can mention the Convent of **La Merced,** the Sanctuary of **Nuestra Señora de la Cinta** and the churches of **San Pedro** and **San Francisco.**

Almonte, Aracena, Ayamonte, Cortejana, Cumbres Mayores and **Jabugo** are other cities of historical and tourist interest.

In 1964 the **Coto de Doñana** was established as a biological station, five years later it was declared the **Nature Park Entorno de Doñana**. At present it is the largest fauna centre of all Europe and stopping off place for many migratory birds. It has mild temperatures (means of 13ºC in winter and 30ºC in summer). This and the physical structure of moving dunes and marshlands make it a region which attracts over 150 species of birds in the winter. The total area of this Park and the smaller individual parks within its borders, is some 75,000 hectares; it is situated in the southeast of the province of Huelva.

The **Nature Park of Sierra de Aracena and Picos de Aroche** lies to the north of the province, inside the western area of the Sierra Morena. It covers some 184,000 hectares, made up mostly of foothills where slate and quartz predominate, giving the landscape its dark colour. Common to this area are the Iberian lynx and the Iberian black stork.

Beach at Punta Umbria

Piedras River at Lepe

Ayamonte, Sports port

Mouth of the Guadiana River

Landscape in the Sierra de Aracena

Ham curing sheds at Jabugo

Aracena

Cortegana Castle

Aracena

Sierra de Aracena

Canela Beach

Ayamonte

Ayamonte, fishing port

J A E N

The province of Jaen is bordered to the north by the Community of **Castilla La Mancha,** with **Granada** to the south and **Cordoba** to the west. It consists of three distinct geographical areas: the Sierra Morena to the north, the Guadalquivir Valley in the centre and the Sub Betica mountains to the south.

The Atlantic winds, which blow through the Betica Valley, cause the mild climate. Summers are very hot and winters cool on the plains, colder in the higher areas. The city of **Jaen** lies at the junction of the Betica Valley and the Sub Betica mountains, at the meeting point of two regions: **La Campiña** and **Los Montes**, to the north and south respectively

The old Roman city of ***Argui*** had rich silver mines. It was also a fortress town in the Carthaginian empire. In the second Punic war, around 207 BC, it was conquered by **Scipio** and under Roman domination included under the jurisdiction of **Ecija**, becoming a township with the status of *flavia* in the times of the Emperor **Vespasian.**

In 712 AD Jaen was conquered by the Arabs, who changed its old name to **Geen**, from which the present day name is derived. During the period of Muslim Caliphate rule, the city reached its maximum splendour. Once more it was converted to a fortress town and palaces and mosques were built. After the fall of the Caliphate it passed into the hands of the Taifa Kingdom of Seville and later was occupied by the **Almoravids** and the **Almohads.**

Jaen

Cathedral

Interior of the Cathedral

In 1246 the city was ceded to **Ferdinand III** under an agreement signed between the dominion of Granada and the Kingdom of Castile. This would cause part of the Muslim population to leave for other regions under Arab rule. The control of this fortress city was of such strategic importance that it was the decisive factor in the continued Castilian rule of High Andalusia. The province of Jaen played an important part in Spanish history. It has a well-known mountain pass, **Despeñaperros**, which connects the Castilian plateau and Andalusia. **Despeñaperros** was to play an important role in the Battle of Bailen: it became the unsurmountable obstacle for the troops of **Napoleon** on their way south.

The oldest monuments in **Jaen** belong to the Muslim period. The Arab baths date from the beginning of the 11th century, the **Castle of Santa Catalina** was rebuilt after the Reconquest of Spain. Most of its walls stand today, including the Tower of Allegiance and the Chapel of Santa Catalina (built between the 13th to 15th centuries).

A Cathedral was built on the site of the old Mosque. Its sacristy is one of the most important achievements of Spanish Renaissance architecture. Other important religious monuments are the churches of **San Andrés, San Ildefonso** and **Santa Magdalena.**

The provincial museum contains important remains from the Neolithic, Iberian, Roman, Spanish-Arab and Renaissance periods.

Andújar, Baeza, Linares and **Ubeda** are important cities of historical interest.

Cazorla

Cazorla

Belenda

Quesada

The **Nature Park of Sierra de Cazorla, Segura** and **Las Villas** is situated to the north of the province of Jaen. It has an area of more than 200,000 hectares, and it is the largest protected area of Spain. The **Guadalquivir** and **Segura** rivers have their sources in this park and flow into the Atlantic and Mediterranean respectively. 1,300 species of plants, 24 of peculiar to this area of Andalusia, are included in the floral catalogue. There are various species of predators such as the fox, the genet, the marten and many birds of prey. This Park is one of the largest reserves in the Iberian Peninsula for entomological species.

The **Nature Park of Sierra Magina** lies in the **La Campiña** area and extends 20,000 hectares over the highest massif of this province (2,167 m). Here we find floral species unique to this area, adapted to the strong winds, low temperatures and high altitude.

Mountain range of Cazorla

Indigenous trees and waterfall, Cazorla

Landscape at Ubeda

Olive groves at Cazorla

Nature Park of Sierra de Cazorla

Sierra de Cazorla

Parador Nacional, Jaen

Parador Nacional entrance

Baeza

Baeza, Palace of Jabalquinto

Cazorla

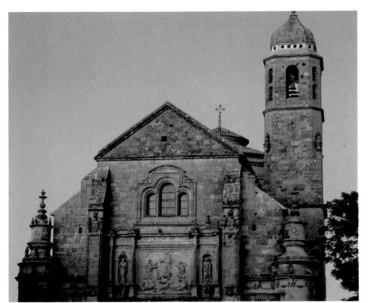
Church of El Salvador, Ubeda

Church of San Miguel, Andujar

Church of San Pablo, Ubeda

Church of San Pablo, Ubeda

Park at Ubeda

Baeza, interior of the Cathedral

M A L A G A

Malaga has boundaries with **Seville** and **Cordoba** to the north, **Granada** to the east and **Cadiz** to the west; to the south, **Malaga** lies on the Mediterranean. Its climate is Mediterranean with mild winters,12°C, and hot summers with mean temperatures of 25°C.

Many traces of prehistoric cultures as far back as the Bronze Age can be found in **Malaga** city itself and its province. The group of burial stones in **Antequera** is the oldest in Europe. The caves at **Nerja** contain prehistoric paintings in black, yellow and red tones.

The origins of the city of **Malaga** date back to the Phoenicians and the Greeks, who founded the colony of **Mainake** near the present city. In 205 BC the town was allied to the Romans, becoming a Roman city under the Emperor **Vespasian.** This city would continue as an important trading centre in spite of the military Roman domination. It exported oil, cereal, wood, salted foods, raisins and wines and the region was a trading centre in slaves.

View of Málaga, taken from the Gibralfaro castle

The Park, Málaga

Málaga Town house

The "Cenachero"

Customs house, 18ᵗʰ c

Condes de Buenavista Mansion, Picasso Museum, Málaga

Plaza de la Merced. Museum Casa Natal Picasso

Museum Casa Natal Picasso

The Alcazaba, Málaga

Patio in the Alcazaba

Interior of the Alcazaba

The Alcazaba and the Gibralfaro Castle

Roman theatre, by the Alcazaba

City walls Gibralfaro castle

Gibralfaro castle

Cathedral

Cathedral

Interior of the Cathedral, Central nave

Choir stalls, Pedro de Mena

Bishop's palace

Church of the Sacristy

Choir stalls

Bishop's palace, interior patio

La Piedad

69

Beach La Malagueta Sea promenade, Paseo Marítimo Pablo Ruíz Picasso

Municipal Museum, Málaga

La Malagueta looking west

Easter week: Semana Santa

The Fair, Málaga

The Fair, Málaga

Malaga developed its trade under the Jews and the Syrian traders When the city was taken from the Byzantines by the Visigoth King **Leovigildo** in 570, trade continued between the Jewish and Spanish-Roman colonies and the north of Africa, Italy, Greece and Asia Minor.

Abd-al-Aziz conquered the city in 714–716 AD. Under the new Caliphate, Malaga became one of the *Khoras,* or territorial areas, of Al-Andalus. It became very prosperous in this period. Its population grew to 15,000 inhabitants at the end of the 10th century, with an urban bourgeoisie composed mainly of Jews and Muladies. After the first **Taifas** and the invasions by the **Almoravids** and the **Almohads** the area became part of the Kingdom

Torremolinos

Historic - Botanic Gardens, La Concepción

Torremolinos

of Granada and the main port of this Kingdom. In 1487 it was conquered by the **Catholic Monarchs, Ferdinand** and **Isabella,** who granted the city its own charter of laws and at the same time re-established its commercial relations with the north of Africa.

During the 16th century **Malaga** and **Alicante** were the two main Mediterranean ports for the export of wool from Castile. The Moorish revolts in 1501 and 1586, their expulsion around 1611, and a general decline of the Spanish economy during the 17th c contributed to a notable decline in commerce which passed into the hands of the English and Dutch. It was not until the 18th century that this area began to recover its trading activity.

The centre has the remains of a Roman theatre and the **Alcazaba** built on the same site in the Arab reign; this latter is joined to the **Gibralfaro fortress** by a long passageway. The Cathedral of Malaga was first built on the site of a major Mosque, but in 1528 a new Cathedral, with three very high naves was started. Other Churches of interest are **El Sagrario**, **Virgen de la Victoria** and the Episcopal Palace. In the archaeological museum of the Alcazaba remains of prehistoric, Roman and Mediterranean cultures can be seen.

Costa del Sol is the name given to the 300 kms. of Mediterranean coastline of the province of **Malaga.** This southern trip of coastline lies at the foot of the Serrania de Ronda

Torre del Mar.

Torrox costa.

Torrox costa.

Velez-Malaga castle

General view of Frigiliana

Typical Morisco Street

Plaza de Nerja.

Paseo del Balcón de Europa. Nerja.

Coast at Nerja, eastern area of the province of Malaga

Statue of Alfonso XII, Balcón de Europa

Panoramic view of Burriana beach, Nerja

and Sierra Nevada, running from Estepona to Motril in the province of Granada. In the early sixties these sunny beaches saw the beginning of the tourist industry boom, which resulted in the building of many hotels, restaurants, nautical ports, holiday resorts etc.

Of historic and tourist interest are the towns of **Antequera, Estepona, Fuengirola, Marbella, Mijas, Nerja, Ronda, Torremolinos and Velez-Malaga.**

The **Nature Park Montes de Malaga** lies to the north of the city. It has an area of 5,000 hectares, re-forested with pines in the basin of the river Guadalmedina as a preventive measure against the flooding which for centuries devasted the capital in the rainy season.

The **Nature Park Sierra de las Nieves** is situated in the Serrania of Ronda. It has an area of over 18,000 hectares and the main morphological characteristics are the gorges of more than 100 metres and abysses which reach a depth of 1,100 m. **La Torrecilla**, the highest point in this park (1,919 m) is situated in the **Sierra de Tolox.** Some 3,000 hectares of the **Sierra de las Nieves** Park are covered with a type of silver fir, the *Pinsapo*, a species only be found in the Sub Betica mountains and in the north of Africa.

Casa Ayo on the Burriana Beach

Parador Nacional at Nerja

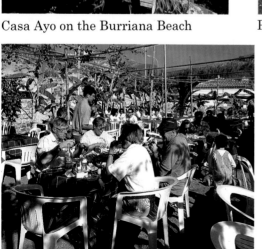
Gastronomic dishes

Paella on the Burriana Beach at Nerja

Puerta Marina. Benalmadena

Benalmadena

Benalmadena

Bil-Bil Castle, Beach at Benalmadena

Sports on the Costa del Sol

Mijas

Beaches at Fuengirola

Fuengirola

Fuengirola

Marbella, Panoramic view of the city, promenade, Sports marina

Paseo Marítimo promenade

La Fontanilla beach

Avenida del Mar

La Fontanilla beach

Paseo de la Alameda.

Castle and city walls, Marbella. Plaza de la Iglesia

Church of Santa María de la Encarnación,18th c

Puerto Banús. Marbella

Typical Andalusian architecture,   Puerto Banús, Marbella

Los Monteros Golf Course, Marbella

Estepona, seafront promenade

Estepona, exceptional hotel infrastructure

Tajo de Ronda

Church of Santa Maria La Mayor, Ronda

Typical shop in Ronda

Bullring at Ronda

Antequera

Casares

Leisure Port, Manilva

SEVILLA

The boundaries of the province of **Seville** are as follows: Badajoz to the north, Cordoba to the east, Malaga to the southeast, Cadiz to the south, and Huelva to the west. The physical structure is conditioned by the basin of the Guadalquivir River, which crosses the whole province to the Atlantic Ocean. The climate is Mediterranean, with average temperatures of 16°C to 18°C, and long hot summers with high levels of humidity.

Archaeological remains here go back to the Neolithic Age. The city's history starts with the Iberian *Turdetano* tribes. **Seville** was later colonized by the Phoenicians, Greeks and Carthaginians, who laid the foundations for its trade development. Around 205 BC the Romans conquered this area; in 48 BC **Scipio *the African*** founded Italica . **Caesar** named it the capital of Betica, making *Hispalis* (Seville) a Roman colony. **Augustus** granted it the privilege of minting coins. Germanic invaders settled here, first the Vandals, then the *Sueves*, and in 513 it was incorporated into the Visigoth Kingdom. In 712 the Muslims reconquered Seville and who renamed it **Isbiliya,** which is the origin of its present name. The city underwent many urbanistic changes, and under the first **Almohad** rule, the great Mosque and its minaret, the **Giralda,** were built (1172 – 1182).

In the reign of the **Catholic Monarchs** a new age of splendour began for **Seville**. This would continue throughout the reigns of **Carlos V** and **Felipe II**. The Cathedral was built and the first Crown printers established at the University.

Plaza de España

La Giralda

Plaza de los Naranjos, Seville

The Royal Citadel

Interior, the Royal Citadel

Gardens of the Royal Citadel

La Cartuja from the Barqueta Bridge

Ceramic decoration, Plaza de España

Gardens of Maria Luisa

The Plaza de España Square

The city was well ahead in the fields of industry and the arts; its development and its eventually becoming the major city of the Kingdom, was due to its port. The port of **Seville** was the point of departure and arrival of all the expeditions to the New World, especially once the ***Casa de la Contratación de las Indias*** (the Trading house for the Americas) was created in 1503. **Seville** became in a way the centre of the world, its original population growing to 150,000 in 1588. However, in the Plague of 1649 around 60,000 died in **Seville** capital and in 1707 the Casa de la Contratación de las Indias was transferred to Cadiz, causing a decline: Seville would only start to recover in the beginning of the 19th century.

The oldest historic remains of the city date from the Muslim period. The **Torre del Oro** and its sister tower, built on the opposite bank of the Guadalquivir, formed part of the

Interior views of the Cathedral

defence system of the fluvial port. In those times, these two towers could be joined by a chain barrier and thus prevent any enemy ships from reaching the port.

The **Giralda,** the old minaret of the original Mosque, is 117m high and looks out over the city, standing as a complement to the Cathedral's beauty. The Cathedral was built on the site of the old Mosque, its style is late Gothic and in size it is only surpassed by St Peter's in Rome and St. Paul's in London. Building was started in 1401, the sculptured altarpiece of its main chapel is the largest in Spain. There are a great number of religious monuments, more notable for their paintings and sculptures than their architecture. Among these are the Church of **El Sagrario,** the Temple of **El Salvador,** the Church of **Santa** Ana, the Temple of **La Magdalena,** the Church of **San Lorenzo,** the Convent of **Santa Paula.**

La Cartuja, interior

One of the Expo buildings

Patio in the Santa Cruz neighbourhood

Juan de Austria fountain

Gardens of Maria Luisa

Seville, Guadalquivir River

The Cathedral, Seville

Of the civil buildings, the Town Hall, which was built in the reign of **Carlos V**, is worthy of mention; so too are the **Hospital de la Caridad**, built in 1647, **the Hospital de los Venerables,** from the 15th century and the **Hospital de la Sangre.** Under the rule of of King **Felipe II,** the **Lonja de Mercaderes** (the Merchant and Trading house) was built between 1572 and 1598; here the Indian Archives on the newly discovered American lands were kept during the reign of **Carlos III.** The most important documents of the conquest and colonization of the Americas are still here, and others are to be found in the Columbus library. Another building from the same time is the Tobacco Factory (**Fábrica de Tabaco,** now one of the University buildings. The **Casa de Pilatos** from the 16th century contains many examples of Roman archaeology. We have the **Palacio de las Dueñas**, from the 15th century and **Palacio de San Telmo** from the same time, originally joined with the **Maria Luisa** Gardens. The most representative example of popular architecture is the old **Barrio de Santa Cruz**, the Jewish Quarters, a labyrinth of narrow streets in the centre of the city.

Roman Arena at Italica

Mosaics, Italica

La Cartuja

The Torre del Oro

La Giralda

Of the museums of **Seville**, the Museum of Fine Arts deserves special mention: it has the second largest collection of paintings in Spain, after El Prado Museum in Madrid. The Provincial Museum of Archaeology contains examples of Roman busts, ceramics, mosaics and Medieval archaeology; the Museum of Contemporary Art contains 20th century work.

Cities of historic and tourist interest in the province of **Seville** are **Alcalá de Guadaira, Carmona, Cazalla, Dos Hermanas, Ecija, Osuna** and **Utrera.**

The **Nature Park of Sierra Norte** lies north of Seville and extends through the Park of **Sierra Morena.** It has an area of over 165,000 hectares of smooth hills with beautiful pasture lands and evergreen oaks, cork trees and holm oaks. The black stork and the Imperial eagle are representative species of the fauna of this park.

Carmona

Sunflowers

Carmona

El Garrobo

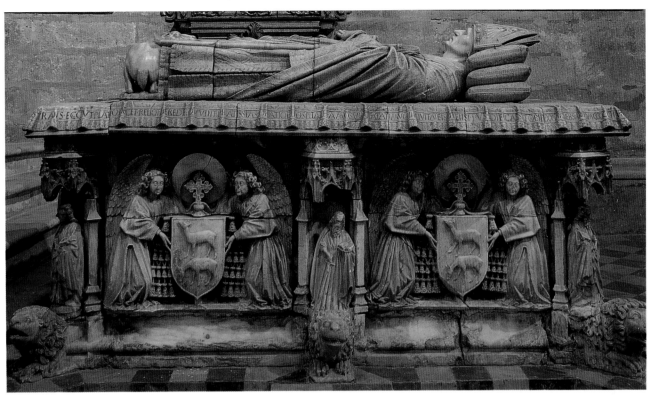

Catedral of Seville, interior

Convent of La Encarnacion, Osuna

Osuna

Facade of the Cabildo Eclesiástico

Interior of the La Colegiata, Osuna

Patio in the La Encarnación Convent

Interior, La Colegiata, Osuna

Seville

Seville

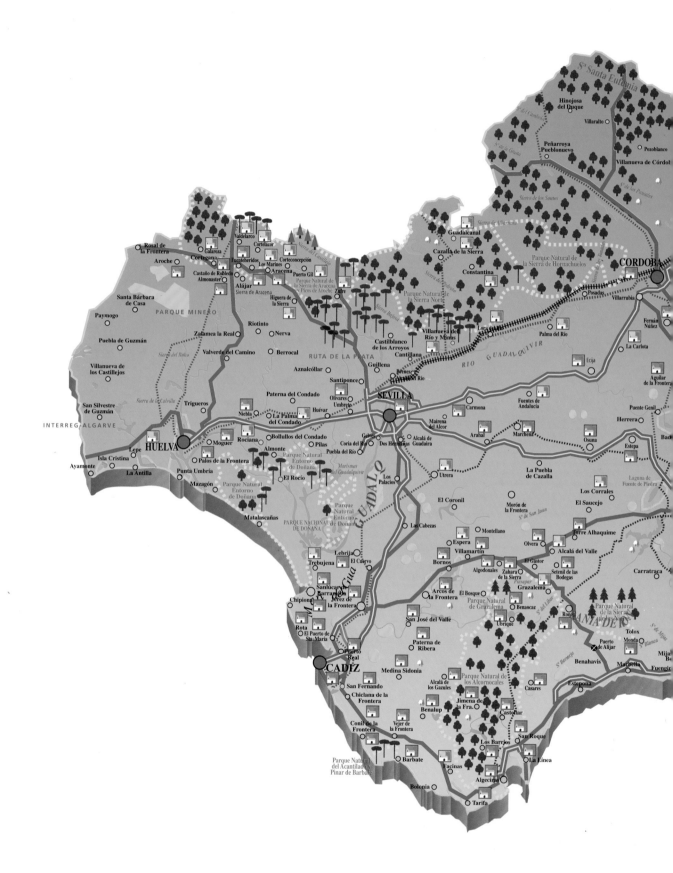